SMILE. BREATHE. LISTEN.

SMILE. BREATHE. LISTEN.

THE 3 MINDFUL ACTS FOR LEADERS

Steve Gladis, Ph.D.
Author of *Positive Leadership: The Game Changer at Work*

ISBN-13: 9780692625958
ISBN-10: 069262595X
Library of Congress Control Number: 2016901614
CreateSpace Independent Publishing Platform
North Charleston, South Carolina

DISCLAIMER

This book attempts to offer research about smiling, breathing, and listening, which I use to inform, motivate, and inspire leaders. It is presented with the understanding that neither I nor the publisher is engaged in rendering any type of psychological, legal, or any other kind of professional advice.

Regarding the fictional case study contained in the book, all names, characters, places, and incidents are products of the author's imagination or are used fictionally. Any resemblance to actual persons (living or dead), businesses, organizations, events, or locales is entirely coincidental.

DEDICATION

This book is dedicated to my wife, Donna Sheehan Gladis, who is a natural at Smile. Breathe. Listen. I can only aspire to her natural capacity for mindfulness.

ACKNOWLEDGMENTS

To Beth Cabrera, Ph.D., my friend and colleague at George Mason University, for reawakening me to mindfulness; Paul M. Jones, M.D., for teaching me Mindfulness-Based Stress Reduction (MBSR) at Georgetown University; and to test-readers of the manuscript (in alphabetical order): Beth Cabrera, Mark Cabrey, Dan Clendenin, Fran Craig, Lisa Dunaway, Kevin Hartigan, Susan Horn, Sara Jaffe, Pio Juszkiewicz, Julie Linkins, Krista Mathis, Dean McIntyre, Terrance Moran, Amanda Moxham, Angela Penn, Jim Price, Dori Ramsey, Lauren Semper-Scott, Gary Sheehan, Anne Steen, and Kourtney Whitehead.

TABLE OF CONTENTS

EXECUTIVE SUMMARY: SMILE. BREATHE. LISTEN.

As a busy executive, you might think you don't even have the hour it takes to read *Smile. Breathe. Listen: The 3 Mindful Acts for Leaders*. Here are some highlights that might just encourage you to read the entire book or at least recommend it to your team.

SMILE.

- We are hard-wired to smile. We're even smiling in the womb. Kids smile like crazy, and mirror neurons allow us to "catch" smiling from others.
- Smiling is good for your long-term health and for a longer and more engaged life.
- Smiling reduces stress, helps us work better, and makes people want to be around us.
- The "Duchenne" smile—a smile that engages the muscles of the eyes as well as those of the mouth—is viewed as genuine and authentic.
- Smiling makes us appear more likable, courteous, and competent.
- Leaders who smile put people at ease, spread positive emotions like a virus, and create an environment in which people can do their best work.

BREATHE.

- Breathing is automatic. However, leaders who understand how to control their breathing will be much more effective.
- Mindful Breathing is the "Big Switch" that helps us move from mental rumination or anxious thinking to more a more thoughtful, relaxed state.
- Mindfulness-Based Stress Reduction (MBSR) is a research-based, highly successful program based on mindful breathing and consistent, regular practice.
- Regularly sitting or lying quietly starts the "practice" of mindfulness.
- The impact of mindful breathing can be seen in our personal, team, and corporate health.
- Leaders who learn mindful breathing not only help themselves become better people but also help those around them to do the same.

LISTEN

- Listening is a skill possessed by the very best leaders.
- Listening represents an important gift that every leader can give—a leader's time and attention are highly valued by those around the leader.
- Good listening consists of presence, technique, and practice.
- Presence is demonstrated when leaders are fully engaged, focused, and not distracted when talking to people.
- The Speaker-Listener Technique focuses on the listener fully understanding the speaker's concerns.
- The Ladder of Inference demonstrates how anyone, including leaders, can jump to conclusions based on their own often erroneous assumptions and beliefs.

- Despite a prodigious amount of data and statistics about how important listening is, a number of leaders—in business, medicine, and any other profession—have poor listening skills.
- Unfortunately, the prognosis for whether people will become more focused, better listeners is not good, because of technology intrusions (emails, texts, phone calls) vying for our immediate attention.

Now, if you have an hour, enjoy the book.

INTRODUCTION

Have you ever seen the movie *The Karate Kid?* To refresh memories and set the context, here's a summary pieced together from The Internet Movie Database, better known as IMDb:

> *Daniel and his mother move from New Jersey to California. She has a wonderful new job, but Daniel quickly discovers that a dark-haired Italian boy with a Jersey accent doesn't fit into the blond surfer crowd. Daniel manages to talk his way out of some fights, but he is finally cornered by several who belong to the same karate school. As Daniel is passing out from the beating he sees Miyagi, the elderly gardener leaps into the fray and save him by outfighting a half-dozen teenagers. Miyagi and Daniel soon find out the real motivator behind the boys' violent attitude. Miyagi promises to teach Daniel karate and arranges a fight at the all-valley tournament some months off. When his training begins, Daniel doesn't understand what he is being shown. Miyagi seems more interested in having Daniel paint his fences and wax cars than in teaching him karate.*[1]

Daniel learns something without knowing it when Miyagi demonstrates the wax-on-wax off techniques of polishing a car. What seems like useless practice of waxing several of Miyagi's cars turns into a powerful lesson. In fact, I would call it mindful muscle building. Mindfulness experts like professors Jon Kabat-Zinn and Mark Williams would call it the "formal practice" that eventually serves young Daniel well and pays off for him in a big way.

THE 3 MINDFUL ACTS

There are three physical exercises, what I call "The 3 Mindful Acts," that leaders or anyone can practice to get in tune with those they lead. These acts might at first seem like the futile wax-on/wax-off exercises that Daniel experienced. However, it turns out that there's a science behind these mindful acts. When practiced and cultivated, the acts produce effective and resonant leaders.[2]

What are these acts? Simply put they are: Smile. Breathe. Listen.

These acts may seem simple, even elicit a big "duh" from some readers, but when you understand their complexity and the science behind them, you might well view them as absolute imperatives for any leader, especially a new one the company is onboarding. Having coached many leaders, including very experienced CEOs and C-level executives, I now know how critical The 3 Mindful Acts are to a leader's success and significance.

Before we explore the 3 Mindful Acts in depth, let's take a moment here to discuss the difference between success and significance. Perhaps one of the most famous painters got it straight. Pablo Picasso once said: "The meaning of life is to find your gift. The purpose of life is to give it away." Indeed, to summarize what John Maxwell, noted leadership author, would say about success and significance: Success is something you may do for yourself, but significance comes when you do it for someone else. The ultimate success in life is causing the success of another.[3] To have a successful, meaningful life we all need to have a purpose. A growing body of positive psychology contends that doing good by helping another moves us from simple happiness to a purpose-driven life.[4] We get to that purpose when we're calm, focused, and attending to others as well as ourselves. And, nothing gets us there faster than The 3 Mindful Acts for Leaders.

THE STRUCTURE OF THE BOOK

This book is intentionally structured to help you be able to

- Understand a review of research relevant to the impact that the practice of "smile, breathe, listen" can have on leaders.
- Observe that research demonstrated in a case study.
- Grasp several key takeaways you can apply to your leadership situation.
- Do some personal reflection.

ABOUT THE CASE STUDY

The fictional case study is embedded in the text as a story. It's presented as a story for a reason. Famed Stanford professor Albert Bandura has pointed out in his research the power such stories, both real and fictional, have on people's learning.

Much like we all, as kids, learned lasting truths from Aesop fables such as the story of the tortoise and the hare, we can likewise learn valuable lessons from business fables. It's worth noting that the *Harvard Business Review (HBR)* uses this very technique to introduce scenarios and then offer potential solutions by experts. Here's how the *HBR* explains its use of case studies: "*HBR*'s fictionalized case studies present dilemmas faced by leaders in real companies and offer solutions from experts."[5]

The business story presented in this book offers a mosaic of various cases and problems I have encountered in working with executives over the years. Thus, while the story and its characters are fictional, the narrative demonstrates the types of real problems that leaders deal with every day.

So let's explore each act—how to:

Smile. Breathe. Listen.
The 3 Mindful Acts for Leaders

ACT:1

SMILE.

We smile, even in the womb! The technology of 3D sonograms has actually shown fetuses smiling! What's more, even blind children will smile at the sound of another human voice. Smiling is hardwired into our brains.[6] And if you're a leader, smiling becomes a key factor for not only your performance but also for that of everyone around you. And while smiling is something most of us do every day, if you've never heard of the Duchenne Smile, chances are you might not know how to smile effectively.

Preview: In the following section, we'll explore research on the biochemistry of smiling, the effects of smiling on those around us as leaders, and the types of smiles.

RESEARCH ABOUT SMILING

As a leader, one of the most primal, easiest, and effective physical acts we can perform is to smile. Here's why: When you meet a new person or have any new experience, your brain—your primal/ reptilian brain—evaluates the person and the situation quickly: in about one-fifth of a second! How? By using a small almond-shaped structure in the brain called the amygdala, the Greek word for almond.

The amygdala is the brain's smoke-detector. It's always on, day or night. You experience it functioning when you wake up from a deep sleep to an unusual sound at night or to the sudden cry of a child. Or, you feel the amygdala at work warning you when you unconsciously swerve away from a car that's invaded your highway lane. The amygdala goes off many times a day—it's never off duty. It's truly the handmaiden of evolution. Without the amygdala, we'd be far more vulnerable to extinction.

The biochemistry that the amygdala produces is complex but is triggered by an inciting stimulus, such as a new CEO scowling during a briefing or a supervisor cross-examining an employee about an error in a spread sheet. The amygdala warns us immediately by screaming "THREAT!" In either case, the scowling CEO or the cross-examining supervisor, the amygdala sets off a cascade of biochemical reactions. In milliseconds, biochemical substances such as adrenalin and cortisol are released into the bloodstream, preparing the body for fight or flight.

The amygdala's sole purpose is to warn the mind and body of impending threats—real or imagined. In highly anxious people, this structure has a particularly sensitive hair-trigger amygdala, which often misinterprets even the slightest of gestures as being threatening. Unfortunately, when people are uncertain in any way, like when a new manager comes into the picture, they are more susceptible to threat, more anxious, and on higher alert.

On the other hand, when a new leader comes in smiling, the amygdalae of otherwise anxious employees register that perhaps this leader is non-threatening and thus prevent their minds and bodies from going on a biochemical wild goose chase. When a new leader "on-boards" into the company and meets you for the first time with smile, your amygdala takes a breath and gives a sigh of relief, at least for the moment. And when the new leader engages you in friendly discussion—for example, asks you to tell him or her what you do or asks about your family and what your interests might be—the amygdala still stays on semi-alert but takes an important breather. Why? Because smiling is a universally accepted signal that this situation is not a hostile but a friendly one.

EFFECTS OF SMILING

Neuroscience suggests that smiling is the fastest way to connect with another person. Because of what are called "mirror neurons," a relatively new discovery in primates, our brains get stimulated and mimic the activities of others—especially actions by leaders and people in positions of authority.[7]

Mirror neurons demonstrate the figurative and literal truth of the saying "monkey see, monkey do." As the story goes, Italian researchers studied monkeys by placing electrodes in their brains and recording electrochemical responses. One hot day an Italian neuroscientist was licking an ice cream cone. The other researchers in the laboratory noted that when the scientist lifted the cone to his mouth, the monkey's brain fired up—in the area that controlled the monkey's arm. It was if the monkey were lifting up and licking his own virtual ice cream cone.[8]

This observation led to a host of research supporting the theory that actions trigger "mimicry" in observers. To put this in more concrete language, when you smile, it's almost a certainty that others will smile back because your act of smiling fires up the mirror neurons in their brains and causes them to mimic your action.

Knowing about mirror neurons is especially important, therefore, for leaders or authority figures. Authority itself is a trigger for creating emotional contagion among followers. And emotions spread quickly through a group.[9]

A leader's smile is much like a smile on steroids! If a leader smiles, people tend to smile; however, a scowling leader creates scowling followers.

Here is some background on smiling from the great TED Talk by Ron Gutman: _The Hidden Power of Smiling_[10]:

Gutman notes that adults smile, at most, 20 times a day. However, kids will crack a smile a whopping 400 times a day! Perhaps this is why grandparents prefer to hang around their grandkids more than their own kids. It's just a lot more fun ☺.

Gutman cites some amusing and fascinating studies about how smiling correlates to better health:

- A 30-year longitudinal study performed at the University of California at Berkeley analyzed student photos in an old yearbook. Researchers measured the smiles of those students. They discovered that those with bigger smiles had longer, healthier marriages, scored higher on well-being self-assessments, and were generally happier and more inspirational to others.
- A Wayne State 2010 study of pre-1950 baseball cards compared players who smiled on their baseball card photos to those who didn't. Non-smilers lived, on average, 73 years; smilers, 80 years!
- One British study on smiling found that one smile approximates the stimulation someone's brain would feel if you gave that person many bars of chocolate—or thousands of dollars!
- Smiling reduces epinephrine and cortisol and increases the production of oxytocin and endorphins (much like what's given off in an amorous encounter).
- A Penn State study demonstrated that smiling people are viewed as more likeable, courteous, and even more competent. So, smiling does a LOT for you—more than we ever thought.

Here's a bit more research to reinforce the point:

- Smiling reduces stress. When people were forced to smile or frown using either a pencil or chopstick in their mouths, those forced to smile had lower heart rates and quick stress reduction compared to those forced to frown—according to a 2012 study in the *Journal of Psychological Science*.[11]
- Smiling makes people like you. A 2004 Penn State study revealed that service employees who smiled had a more

positive impact on their customers and got better tips.[12] Research by Michael Lynn at Cornell University also indicates a substantial increase in tips for servers who smiled genuinely at customers.[13]

- Smiling helps you think better. According to research by noted "positive emotions" researcher, Barbara Frederickson (University of North Carolina), people who smiled produced better cognitive performance.[14]

TYPES OF SMILES

Many people smile politely, not necessarily genuinely, often when meeting others in social settings. This smile is called the "Pan Am" smile (Pan Am was the name of a former airline that flew around the world), made famous in a *Saturday Night Live* skit where stewardesses and stewards perfunctorily smiled, waved, and said: "Buh-Bye, Buh-Bye." The sketch was funny because they repeated the Buh-Bye over and over—so insincerely that it became a running gag.

However, there is a smile that we all perceive as authentic and trustworthy: The Duchenne Smile.[15] Discovered by 19th Century French neurologist, Guillaume Duchenne, in this smile, both corners of the mouth turn upward, and the muscles of the eyes, too, contract into "crow's feet."

Thus, to project an authentic smile, the muscles around the mouth *and* the muscles around the eyes must be engaged. (There's actually some complex physiology behind what makes that happen—about 17 different muscles are involved.)

Though we all recognize the difference between the perfunctory "buh-bye" Pan Am smile and the more authentic Duchenne smile (even around the world), there are a few cultural quirks around smiling. For example, too much smiling in Russia and China (and in New York City☺) can be viewed as suspicious.

That said, you can actually "fake it till you make it." Faking smiling can lead to more positive emotions. According to Harvard professor Amy Cuddy in her now famous <u>TED Talk</u>, even when we don't feel positive or confident, if we push ourselves to exhibit positive, even "winning" attitudes, we become more positive, more prone to smile, and more confident and powerful.[16]

Bottom Line: Smile. It's good for you and anyone around you, especially if you're a leader. It is contagious and leads to positive outcomes.

INTRODUCTION TO THE STORY: STRATEGIC PARTNERS

The following story is a fictional case study based on various situations and problems I've observed as a result of coaching executives over the years. And while the story and the main characters are fictional, they are dealing with realistic problems that leaders face every day.

THE CHARACTERS

J.C. (John Cameron) Williams: J.C. is a 40-year-old master executive coach, and a former professor at the Darden Business School at the University of Virginia (UVa). He's cool, calm, and resolute. After a bout with lymphatic cancer, J.C. re-evaluated his life and decided his mission in life would be to become an executive coach.

Sophia Diaz: Only 29 years old and a Stanford Business School standout, Sophia had moved to Fairfax, Virginia, to accept an associate professorship at George Mason University. Modest, easy-going, and unaware of her own attractiveness, Sophia wears a permanent smile. She has formed a consulting company (Diaz-Kirk) with her associate, Mark Kirk, whom she met at an executive conference in Aspen.

Mark Kirk: Intelligent and hard charging, Mark's a Harvard B-school whiz kid. At 35 he'd already established and sold his second company, MRK Consulting, which was focused on corporate financial growth. Mark is the "alpha dog" in most business settings, which works both for and against him. He's the antithesis of Sophia.

THE SITUATION

Sophia and Mark have formed a partnership, Diaz-Kirk, and while they have been successful in the first year of their partnership, Sophia wants J.C. to coach her and Mark, who can be a good guy one minute and then an arrogant jerk the next—but always amazingly brilliant.

Mark reluctantly agrees to work with J.C. as their coach. The first couple of meetings are a kind of jousting match, with Mark trying to establish his "alpha dog" position, but J.C. intelligently parrying Mark's arrogance. In private, Sophia has some harsh words with Mark about being in or out of this partnership and eventually Mark acquiesces to the coaching.

J.C. meets with them each individually weekly for one-hour one-on-ones. In addition, the three of them meet in a 90-minute joint session every two weeks without fail, without compromise.

In one of the early joint sessions, J.C. has each of them say what they like about the other. Mark says that he admires Sophia's generosity and how she savors life. Sophia says that she admires Mark's world-class brain and his loyalty. Then the two are asked by J.C. to give a wish to each other. Mark wishes that Sophia trusted people more—she'd been very hurt by an unfaithful fiancée. Sophia wishes that Mark would stop trying to always impress people, especially his Dad—a larger-than-life figure in Mark's life. Mark gets angry and storms out.

But, Mark comes back to the next session and all the following sessions. What follows is their story: Strategic Partners.

———

THE STORY ~ ACT 1: SMILE.

J.C. took a sip of water and then said to Sophia and Mark, who were seated on the couch, "Next, I want to let you both in on a secret if you can handle that. OK?" He looked at them each individually, and they both nodded, though Mark more slowly than Sophia.

J.C. settled back in his big leather chair. He talked about having gone to Harvard, then Oxford on a Rhodes scholarship, and all the personal arrogance that came with that heady wine. And being the youngest professor at UVa's Darden School of Business only added to his feeling of "owning the world." Then, the cancer came. The fear of the unknown, the chemo, the weight loss, the loss of hair, and his diminished physical confidence. Finally, even the loss of Big Walt, his dad and best friend. All this had humbled J.C.

One of the last things Big Walt, a nationally known journalist, had taught J.C. was what Walt called "The 3 Mindful Acts" of leadership he learned as a journalist and an editor.

"There are three simple, mindful, and powerful acts all leaders can perform to elevate their game to the next level—from success to significance," J.C. said.

Both Sophia and Mark leaned forward, waiting for the rest of what J.C. was going to say.

J.C. paused to take a sip of water, building up the anticipation. He explained that success was what you did for yourself. "Success gets us skills, promotions, salaries, recognition. And it's all about you the individual."

But, he explained, significance was all about how you used your skills, knowledge, and training to contribute to the success of others and help them make a difference in the world.

"Success without significance—without meaning and purpose in the world—," he said, "will leave you selfish, empty, and petty."

Then he told them another quick story. "Do you remember the book *Eat, Pray, Love?*"

Sophia nodded. Mark said he'd heard of it.

J.C. gave them a quick summary. He explained that while in her thirties, the author Elizabeth Gilbert had decided to leave her marriage and the United States, on a kind of sabbatical in search of her soul. She traveled to Italy to find the delights of *la dolce vita*, the sweet life, and the wonderful food there. After completing the "Eat" phase of her voyage, she traveled to India, where she learned to meditate and calm her inner frantic mind, a second phase that she considered the "Pray" leg of her journey. Finally, she found "Love" in Bali, on the third leg of her journey.

J.C. let the story sink in. Then he drew the link between Gilbert's story and Walt's secret message.

"We all have to go on our own journey—like Gilbert did. There's just no escaping it—the journey must be taken—or we never get there," J.C. said, looking them each in the eye.

J.C. explained that being mindful meant that people, especially leaders, had to be fully present, aware, and non-judgmental—fully in the game. Then he said, "If it's OK, I'd like to describe the first of 'The 3 Mindful Acts.'"

Two enthusiastic nods.

"OK, the first Act that leaders can perform is—drumroll, please—SMILE."

Both of them just laughed.

"Sounds like such a trivial thing, but smiling is THE fastest way for humans to connect," J.C. said. "Nothing else even comes close."

J.C. explained that there was a ton of science behind smiling and even recommended a TED Talk by Ron Gutman, a Silicon Valley executive involved in healthcare: "The Hidden Power of Smiling." This less-than-ten-minute-presentation is packed with study after study that helps make his case that smiling is the best thing you can do for yourself and others. J.C. also mentioned research from several other sources that showed how smiling was "contagious" and spread immediately through newly discovered "mirror neurons," and how it lowered blood pressure, helped you live longer, and even made you appear competent and confident.

"What the heck are mirror neurons?" Mark asked.

J.C. told them how we all have neurons that mimic what others around us do, especially if we identify with them. He explained how we all "catch" the emotions and actions of others. "So, when someone starts to cry, it makes us feel sad. And when someone starts laughing, we catch that feeling and tend to copy it—all the work of mirror neurons," J.C. said.

"Wow! So, monkey-see-monkey-do is true!" Mark blurted.

"Indeed it is," said J.C.

Sophia laughed at Mark's observation and cleared her throat. In a few seconds later Mark cleared his throat. She pointed at him and said, "Monkey see, monkey do!" and they all had a good laugh.

When things settled down, J.C. went on to describe the difference between a fake and an authentic smile. He explained that sometimes when you see people, you flash them a quick fake smile—done with the lips alone. It's quick, unemotional, and only involves the muscles of the mouth. However, he said, a French researcher named Duchenne spent a lot of time studying fake vs. authentic smiles and found that when people smile authentically, not only do the mouth muscles get involved in creating the smile, the muscles around the eyes also crinkle and form "crows' feet."

"And that's how you can tell a real from a fake smile. Pretty simple and most of us know this stuff instinctively. Duchenne just proved it," J.C. said smiling, and pointing to the crows' feet at the corners of his eyes.

Sophia jumped in. "And I always thought crows' feet were a sign of aging."

J.C. shot back, "Aging well—the sign of a good life."

"Well put," said Mark.

J.C. glanced at the clock on the wall across from him and realized he'd kept them there about ten minutes longer than he should have.

"OK, I apologize for keeping you over the time."

"Hey, what a fun session," Sophia said, and Mark nodded in agreement.

"OK, here's your homework assignment: First, smile a lot. In the beginning, it might feel awkward. Just know that kids smile 400 times a day but adults only 20 times a day—who do you think is happier?! Second, put a yellow sticky note on your desk with a smiley face on it and move it around every day as a reminder to practice smiling. Third, keep notes in your journal about the impact your smiling has on you and others around you—note how other people respond. And be ready to report back next time."

Sophia smiled back at him pointing to her crows' feet. And both Mark and J.C. smiled back.

The next couple of weeks went by fast and again, the two individual meetings had a different flavor—more congeniality, a looser feel, even with Mark. And, as before, their individual practices with smiling were of two different flavors.

Mark actually spent a lot of time in front of the mirror practicing the Duchenne smile. He quickly realized that you really had to get your whole face into the smile. It helped him to think of something really funny. What's more, the practice of thinking about funny stuff and then watching his own smile actually made him smile more and that made him happier. He began to prop up his iPhone and filmed himself practicing. For Mark it was all about drill and practice.

On the other hand, Sophia really didn't need to do practice anything. She was a natural smiler with a great outlook on life to begin with. She just kept doing more of the same. However, she did start making notes of how other people smiled and could intuitively tell when people were faking it by looking for crows' feet around their eyes.

When the partner session started and J.C. sat down, Sophia said, "OK, Mark, on three. One, two, three!" They both smiled in unison—the Duchenne smile!

"Wow! Talk about making my day!" said J.C., noticing that they were a lot happier than he'd ever seen them before.

J.C. then asked them how the week went. Mark noted that at first smiling on purpose felt weird and even unnatural for him, but that after a few days, he started to catch the spirit of it all. He'd noticed that, for example, when he went into Peet's Coffee at Kings Park on the way to work, he started smiling more and the friendly folks behind the counter engaged with him even more than usual. At work, he began to test his smile on colleagues and clients with the same results—when he smiled, so did they. Smiling lightened the tone of meetings. And, when he reviewed his journal, he noticed that the smiling had made a significant impact on him, particularly his attitude.

Sophia started by smiling and saying how much more fun it was working with Mark now that they were both smiling more. Mark smiled back and actually blushed. Her journaling had mostly been around how well Mark and she were getting along and how much she appreciated the atmosphere, especially with clients, around the workplace. And she'd put up a handwritten poster in the conference room that screamed "SMILE!"

"Well, I'd say you both would make Professor Duchenne very pleased indeed," J.C. said. "OK. I think you two are ready for the second big act—Breathe."

KEY TAKEAWAYS FROM ACT 1: SMILE.

- We are hard-wired to smile. We're even smiling in the womb. Kids smile like crazy, and mirror neurons make us catch smiling from others.
- Smiling is good for your long-term health, a longer life, and a more engaged one.
- Smiling reduces stress, helps us work better, and makes people want to be around us.
- The "Duchenne" smile is viewed as genuine and authentic.
- Smiling makes us appear more likable, courteous, and competent.
- Leaders who smile put people at ease, spread positive emotions like a virus, and create an environment in which people can do their best work.

REFLECTION AND PRACTICE

- **Answer these questions:**
  - ○ Would you say that, at work, you smile more than you frown?
  - ○ Pick one leader who smiles and one who does not. What are your reactions to each of those leaders?
  - ○ How often do you laugh at work? (Just take a guess.)
  - ○ On a scale from 1–10 (1=low and 10=high), how would you rank your job as being one that makes you smile and have fun?

- **Try these simple exercises:**
  - ○ Before you go into your next meeting, practice the Duchenne smile in the mirror for two minutes. Also, smile deliberately in the meeting.
  - ○ After the meeting, jot down any observations you had about yourself and your attitude in the meeting and how others reacted to your smiling. Did they smile back?
  - ○ Smile authentically at three people today. How did they respond?
  - ○ Put a picture of a smiley face on your computer screen to remind you to smile during your next telephone call. How, if at all, was the energy different on that call?

- **Jot down any thoughts or questions that came from having read this chapter.**
  - ○ _____
  - ○ _____
  - ○ _____
  - ○ _____

ACT:2

BREATHE.

Let's try a simple experiment. Look at a nearby clock. Now hold your breath for 30 seconds or as long as you can until it's uncomfortable for you. Ready, set, go.

Tick, tock…30 seconds later—time's up. Now, breathe!

Were you thinking at all about breathing before you were asked you to hold your breath? If you're like most people who have ever been through this small but powerful exercise in one of my classes, your answer is almost always "No." That's because breathing is automatic and unconscious.

When leaders get upset or nervous, breathing typically accelerates and occurs higher in the chest as the body seeks more oxygen. What's more, such anxious breathing gets telegraphed to people on the leader's team and spreads like a virus—a kind of emotional contagion.

Question: What can stop this vicious cycle?

Answer: Mindful breathing.

So now try this exercise: Close your eyes and just breathe normally for two minutes. Ready, set, go.

Two minutes later…

What happened? What ran through your mind? Any thoughts about the past, present, or even the future? Maybe daydreaming or worrying?

Most people say that they thought of things in the past—something they had done, either good or bad—and/or they thought about future—what they needed to do later that day, the next day, or even the next week or month.

That's how the brain works. We often ruminate about the past or fret about the future. Both, when done to excess, can be the root of either depression or anxiety. Your brain is an amazing tool. (Note: For the purposes of this book, I've used the term "brain" to mean the physical organ and the term "mind" to mean the brain at work—thinking. There's been a debate over the decades about this, but I've adopted these distinctions based on upon what respected researchers say.[17])

Preview: In the following section, we'll explore the neuroscience of breathing, mindful breathing, and the effects of mindful breathing on you, the people you lead, and your organization.

RESEARCH ON BREATHING

The neuroscience behind breathing can get pretty complex. But here's how it works, explained at a layperson's level.

Basic bodily functions like breathing, circulation, neural response, digestion, and others all work without us actively thinking about them or cognitively controlling them. In short, they're all on autopilot (otherwise known as the autonomic nervous system).

The autonomic nervous system is divided into two branches, the sympathetic and parasympathetic nervous systems.

The sympathetic nervous system (SNS) controls the body's fight–flight primal response to any threat. Let's say someone throws a baseball at you when you're not ready, but you catch sight of it at the last moment and duck as you hear it whiz by your ear. That's the SNS at work. If you actually stopped to think— *"Hmm, there's a ball coming my way!"* You'd get beaned!

In more sophisticated situations, when there is time, the SNS engages the prefrontal cortex (PFC), which acts as a kind of firewall between the fast-acting amygdala (the brain's fire alarm) and any actions you might take. Chronic stress, or being in the state of constantly operating in the SNS state, leads to the thinning of the

PFC, the executive function of the brain that helps us make good decisions. Such thinning of the PFC makes you more vulnerable to stress and more likely to be a "carrier" of stress to others, especially if you're a leader. At the same time, chronic stress exacerbates the amygdala, which triggers more stress—elevating blood pressure, increasing stress hormones, and hurting the immune system. Such effects not only have a negative effect on us but also a negative effect on anyone in our proximity.

The PFC (located right behind your forehead) also acts as a kind of "flight simulator," as Harvard's Dan Gilbert[18] calls it, because it can conjure up all sorts of images as our brains try to interpret and actually practice potential acts. It's an evolutionary device to keep us safe. For example, if we watch one person attempt to jump across a puddle and not make it without getting wet, we do a simulation in our own mind to decide whether we'll jump or not.

The second part of the autonomic system, the parasympathetic system (PNS), focuses on the body and switches off the SNS emotional surge, allowing us to consider options under pressure. If the SNS is the fight-or-flight trigger in our brain, then the PNS is the rest-and-recover part of our brain. Psychologist Rich Hanson[19] puts it this way: Triggering the parasympathetic nervous system, often through long slow breathing, switches the mind from fight-or-flight to rest-and-digest as it slows down heart rate, increases intestinal activity, and relaxes muscles in the gastrointestinal tract.

THE BIG SWITCH: MINDFUL BREATHING

Fortunately, we can all take advantage of what I call "The Big Switch": Mindful Breathing. Simply focusing on your breath calms your mind and body. For thousands of years, Eastern monks have been studying the process of focusing on breathing; they call it "meditation." Modern neuroscience and brain scan studies demonstrate that simply being in the present moment, not thinking about the past or the future, and focusing on your breath, calms your mind and allows it to make better decisions. Brain scans and interviews with trained psychologists indicate that meditators, or mindful-breathers, are also among the happiest people in the world.[20]

There's a lesson here for us all. Yet because meditation has been associated with Buddhism, many Westerners treat meditation as some Eastern hocus pocus. Wrong! So, I'd like to adopt a new way of discussing the topic: Mindful Breathing.

MINDFULNESS-BASED STRESS REDUCTION (MBSR)

Over thirty years ago, MIT microbiologist Jon Kabat-Zinn started teaching at the University of Massachusetts Medical School and developed a program to help patients deal with chronic pain. He called it Mindfulness-Based Stress Reduction (MBSR)—an eight-week comprehensive program based on teaching people how to become more present and less distracted by things like pain, obsession, a wandering mind, and much more. The core of the practices he developed (body scan, mindful sitting, mindful movement, and mindful eating)—are all grounded in meditation (mindful breathing)—in other words, concentrating on breathing. Sounds simple, but then so does being able to accurately putt a golf ball, and we all know how tough that skill can be to master without practice!

I completed the MBSR eight-week course offered through Georgetown University's Medical School. It's useful to note that this program is most often offered at medical schools because of its original orientation to the treatment of chronic pain. In fact, there have been hundreds of clinical studies about the program's positive effects.[21]

Indeed, MBSR's popularity has grown dramatically in the past few decades since Kabat-Zinn started the program. Television journalist Anderson Cooper recently attended a program run by Kabat-Zinn and reported it on the popular news program, *60 Minutes*.[22]

THE IMPACT OF MINDFULNESS

Indeed, mindfulness has become popular, and all manner of press tout its many benefits. For example, *New York Times* writer David Gelles recently published a book called *Mindful Work: How Meditation Is Changing Business from the Inside Out.* In his research, Gelles notes the following tangible benefits of meditation[23]:

Impact on the Brain. Meditation (mindful breathing) reduces the size and sensitivity of the amygdala—the brain's fire alarm—as it thickens the prefrontal cortex, the brain's emotional firewall that keeps us from doing or saying stupid things under stress. Mediation increases concentration, self-control, and learning, which have even been documented in school systems.

Impact on Health. Heart attacks, strokes, diabetes, and cancer are exacerbated by an overactive amygdala and the hormones it causes to be released during stress. Meditation has a serious impact on lowering stress levels by lowering heartbeats and inhibiting the amount of cortisol and adrenalin in our systems that can create chronic, inflammatory diseases.

Corporate Impact. Companies like Google, General Mills, Aetna, LinkedIn, Twitter, Goldman Sachs, Genentech, Ford, Cisco, and many others have substantially invested in meditation-based programs to calm executive minds, contributing to better leadership. The practice of mindfulness shows evidence that companies can become more profitable and effective because their employees are less stressed, more adaptive, and more present in the moment.

Sports Impact. Phil Jackson won 11 NBA titles! And he did it using meditation as one of his go-to tools. He taught mindfulness to Michael Jordan, Scottie Pippen, Kobe Bryant, and Shaquille O'Neal. Teaching his pros to breathe and let go of bad shots and botched plays helped his players become resilient. Pete Carroll of the Seattle Seahawks is also using mindfulness with his team.

HOW TO DO MINDFUL BREATHING

Start simple. Developing a mindful breathing practice or plan should be focused on sustainability, and not on anything fancy or overblown. My name for this is a Mindful Breathing Practice. Here's how:

- Sit down, upright, toward the front of the chair. Actively hold yourself erect, and keep your hands on your thighs or hold them gently in your lap.
- Breathe slowly in and then out, and focus on your breathing by thinking "I am breathing in" (when you inhale) and then "I am breathing out" (when you exhale). After a while, you won't need to think about the words; you'll just breathe—in and out.
- Whenever other thoughts swim into your head, like a report that's due or something your husband or wife said at breakfast that bothered you, let those thoughts swim by like fish in the sea. Then, as soon as you can, refocus on your breathing.
- Start to do this for three, five, or ten minutes a day for thirty days, and you'll see things starting to change. Do it for twenty minutes a day for three months, and life starts to change. I can personally testify to this. You will start to become more patient, less reactive, and generally happier and more content with the present—which is the only thing we ever really have at our disposal!
- Now, as our friends at Nike tell us: JUST DO IT!

THE POWER OF 3

As humans, we've always had a fascination with numbers. In fact, numerology is the study of numbers. I'm particularly fond of the number "3." Plays have three acts; baseball has three outs; speeches have three parts. So much in our lives has its basis in the number "3."

In fact, one of the practices in mindfulness is called the three-minute breathing space. Quite simply, it takes just three minutes to become mindful. Follow the mindful breathing instructions offered above, and only do the exercise for three minutes. That's it. You can fit it into any part of your day—which is the great joy and utility of the exercise. Do it before your next big phone call, meeting, or activity at work, at home, or even at play. It's a great transition that clears your mental pallet and prepares and transitions you for what's next in your day.

Too often we jump from one activity to another without benefit of transition. To get good at doing this, set your smartphone timer to three minutes—when I do it, I end with a chime tone that's more subtle than abrupt. Also, I use this technique when I shift to different activities, such as shifting from writing this piece to logging on to a webinar I'm viewing this afternoon, to allow for a better transition.

Transitions are an integral part of our life. I buy a cup of coffee, walk to my car, drive to my office, then show up at an appointment. Sometimes I have to stop at a traffic light, take an elevator, even wash my hands. Some transitions are bigger than others. When the transitions are more involved, such as meeting with one client and then meeting with another, I will often take a three-minute mindful-breathing break. When just transitioning from one activity to another, I'll do a mindful three-breath transition. That's all—just three breaths. That short amount of breathing often is enough to help any transition.

If you've ever seen a baseball player try to scoop up an easy ground ball—but get ahead of himself looking to throw it and then fumble the grounder—you've seen poor transition at play. There is sufficient research about how attempting to multitask significantly degrades the performance of both tasks. Despite all the bravado about multitasking, we can't do it well.[24] Taking a few moments to make sure you've finished one task before shifting to the next is fundamental to success, but not always adhered to in our multi-tasked world.

Now, back to the story: Strategic Partners.

THE STORY ~ ACT 2: BREATHE.

J.C. started again with a story. "When I was a kid, my dad, Big Walt, taught me something he learned at Bethesda Naval Hospital after he got injured in Vietnam."

Walt had been hit with shrapnel from a booby-trapped mortar round that had severed a number of muscles and nerves in both his legs. Initially, the doctors were convinced he would lose both legs, but Walt fought to save them, and he lived to walk again. But the pain was awful. One of the nurses, who had taken a real liking to Walt, taught him how to breathe as a way of controlling the pain!

Mark and Sophia spoke at the same time. "Breathe?"

"Yes, I know—sounds so simple. But breathe in a special, intentional way." J.C. explained that the nurse taught Big Walt how to simply focus on breathing in and breathing out—deliberately, consciously. Many years later, the slow intentional breathing that she taught Walt became one of the most revolutionary pain reduction practices: mindfulness -based stress reduction—also called MBSR. Developed by Dr. Jon Kabat-Zinn, who taught at the University of Massachusetts Medical School, mindfulness helps us all focus on the present.

J. C. quoted Kabat-Zinn's definition: "Mindfulness is all about **paying attention** in a **particular way: on purpose,** in the **present moment,** and **non-judgmentally**." The nurse who helped Big Walt had heard about mindful breathing from soldiers who'd come back from Vietnam. While there, many of them had learned how to "meditate" using the breath as their primary point of reference. When you begin to concentrate on breathing, your brain shifts away from the usual mindless, "monkey brain" we all have that often darts forward toward anxiety or backwards toward sad, depressive memories. And when you're in pain, you get fixated on and anxious about the next wave of pain and that makes it even worse. Walt got pretty good at breathing with the nurse who held his hand as they practiced every day.

"That nurse later became my Mom," J.C. said with a big smile.

"Aww," Sophia said with her hand on her heart. Mark flashed a quick smile.

"Turns out," J.C. explained, "breathing is what I call The Big Switch. When you're in any kind of pain, anger, or distraction, just breathe, slowly and deliberately, and be present wherever you are—not worried about the future or saddened by the past—neither of which you can change. The present is all you really have—right here, right now."

He took a sip of water, then went on to explain how mindful breathing, also called meditation, helped him through all his cancer surgery and the chemo.

"Without it, I think I would have died, seriously. It kept me in the moment. And eventually I grew to see how beautiful the moment is."

J.C. told them that there had been hundreds of convincing clinical studies to prove how effective mindfulness is. Even Anderson Cooper on *60 Minutes* did a story of his own experience learning mindfulness with Jon Kabat-Zinn at an executive retreat.

"In fact, I believe that it's the 'new running,'" J.C. said. "You might remember many years ago when some people started distance running— even running marathons. At first, everyone thought it was crazy and then it caught on and became mainstream. That's where mindfulness is today."

Sophia said, "Whoa—that's very cool!"

J.C. looked at both of them. "You two may want to get mindful—right here, right now," he said. "You'll both need to practice this stuff every day if you want to get in control of your lives, let alone your partnership."

That was when he pulled two copies of Dr. Mark Williams' book, *Mindfulness: An Eight-Week Plan for Finding Peace in a Frantic World,* off his bookshelf and handed each of them a copy.

"Look, you two are at a crossroads," J.C. said. "Your lives can go in various directions. You get to choose. And this book can set you on an amazing course if you practice it. Read a chapter a week and practice the exercises—it takes a couple of months to get fully into a groove. That's it. But the discipline of doing the practices is like taking your mind to the gym—without all the sweat!"

All three of them laughed.

"If you're willing to give this a try and check in every week with me, I can guarantee changes inside each of you and between you both—about how you relate to each other. But frankly, if you decide not to, I'm going to suggest you consider another coach because I'm not sure I can be of great value any more. It's not an ultimatum, but I do know what's possible and not, at least for me as a coach. Think about it and let me know. You both have to agree for me to stay in the relationship. We clear?"

"Clear," said Mark as he took the book.

"Yes, clear," said Sophia.

————

The next couple of weeks were a study in personalities and practice. Not surprisingly, Mark's practice was pretty rigid. Each day at 5:30 A.M., he reached for his iPhone to access the meditation sessions, each about 8–14 minutes long, that Dr. Williams makes available online.

Mark started with the body-scan meditation that gets you breathing slowly as you get in touch with your own body by focusing on your toes, feet, ankles, legs—moving slowly up your body to the top of your head. From the book, Mark learned that the body-scan exercise puts you in present, in a moment-to-moment awareness. Because stress starts in your body, getting familiar with the body is a basic to becoming mindfully present in the moment, not distracted by your thoughts.

As with most things, Sophia was looser about her practice but also performed it every day. Sometimes she meditated it in the morning. Other times she meditated before bed or even during the day on a park bench near her office. One meditation practice she thought was really cool was "mindful movement": walking with her eyes downcast and moving ever so slowly. Shifting weight from one foot to the other at a snail's pace, she was able to get in tune with her body, especially when it was in motion. Later both she and Mark learned that you can do anything "mindfully." In fact, she practiced using her computer mouse as a left-hander. And while it was awkward, she really got into it—and it helped the occasional neck pains she got when she did a lot of writing on her laptop.

Near the end of the month, J.C. could see a bit of a difference between how Mark and Sophia reacted to each other. "So, how's it going with the mindfulness practice?" he asked.

Mark nodded. "OK. I'm sticking with it. No big revelations yet."

Sophia smiled and said, "I'm enjoying it—hasn't made me any prettier but here's hoping!"

J.C. laughed and even Mark cracked a smile.

"How's it going as you work with your clients?"

Mark said working with clients was actually going better. Both he and Sophia had read about taking one breath before entering into a conversation and three breaths if they were upset or nervous. Mark found these techniques particularly helpful.

Sophia chimed in, "I'm not so free-flowing. I breathe, form some thoughts, and then 'publish' them to the public. Hey, now that I talk about it, I think the mindfulness practice is starting to have an effect!" she said with a big smile.

J.C. smiled back at her and said, "That's kinda how it works. The daily practice becomes a kind of new muscle you build. Like doing ab-crunches. You do them today, knowing that when you go to the beach, you'll fit better into your bathing suit!"

"I have a question," Sophia said.

"Go ahead."

"Sometimes, actually a lot, while I'm breathing—meditating—I think about other things. Like what I have to do or thinking about the all I just got from my mother. Random stuff."

"Me too," Mark said.

J.C. explained that part of the brain is a wandering mind, a kind of evolutionary mechanism that keeps us on the lookout for potential threats. However, as you practice mediation more and more, you're able to focus on the moment and calm down the "monkey brain" that darts back and forth and often takes over. He suggested thinking of incoming random thoughts as clouds passing by.

"Notice them, and then gently bring your mind back to the breathing," he said. "As one teacher told me, 'Think of yourself as the sky and these thoughts simply as passing clouds that come and go.' "

"So, I'm not nuts?" Sophia said with a wide grin.

"Not at all, J.C. said.

"Well, sometimes, just a little," Mark said with a smile and a wink.

All three of them laughed.

J.C. continued to ask them a lot of questions about their clients and about issues that had arisen, both with the clients and between the two partners. They had a great exchange with several ah-ha moments in the conversation—typical of a good coaching session.

KEY TAKEAWAYS FROM ACT 2: BREATHE.

- Breathing is automatic. However, a leader who understands how to control her/his breathing will be much more effective.
- Mindful Breathing is the "Big Switch" that helps us switch from mental rumination or anxious thinking to more a more thoughtful, relaxed state.
- Mindfulness-Based Stress Reduction (MBSR) is a highly successful program based on mindful breathing and consistent regular practice.
- Sitting or lying quietly on a regular basis starts the "practice" of mindfulness.
- The impact of mindful breathing can be seen in our health—including personal, team, and corporate health.
- Leaders who learn mindful breathing not only help themselves become better people but also help those around them do the same.

REFLECTION AND PRACTICE

- **Answer these questions**:
  - When you get upset, can you describe what happens inside your body?
  - When you see others get upset, what do you observe?
  - Pick one leader who in your mind is mindful, thoughtful, and in control. How does that person respond to stress?
  - What gets in your way when you get upset? How do you respond?
  - How do you feel when you're relaxed?
  - On a scale from 1 to 10 (1=low and 10=high) how would you rate your level of anxiety and depression?

- **Try these simple exercises**:
  - Pick a particular time of the day, and start meditating, mindful breathing, for just three minutes. It's the consistency, not the duration, that matters most.
  - Connect your own mindful breathing to habits or regular occurrences. For example, at stoplights, instead of being frustrated, use them as one- to two-minute breathing breaks.
  - When switching between tasks at work, take three deep breaths to announce the change to your mind.
  - When practicing mindful breathing, put one hand on your chest and one on your stomach. If you're doing mindful breathing, the hand on your stomach—not the hand on your chest—should be rising and lowering.
  - Before responding to a remark that might upset you, pause and take a few deep breaths. You'll be glad you did!

- **Jot down any thoughts or questions that came from having read this chapter.**

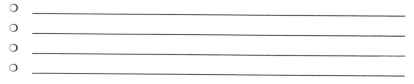

ACT:3

LISTEN.

S tudies show that leaders talk significantly more than others in a given group.[25] Having been an executive coach for a number of years, I have worked with numerous executives from government agencies, non-profits, and privately owned and publicly traded companies. I've worked through all kinds of problems and issues with young and old, men and women. Without question the most important skill that high-performing executives must develop, to be not only successful themselves but also significant to others, is to listen.

Preview: In the following section, we'll explore the research on listening. This research includes information on how to listen and on a phenomenon called "the ladder of inference" that can not only get in the way of good listening but also create big problems in relationships and organizations.

RESEARCH ON LISTENING

For leaders, listening is the Holy Grail.[26] Discovering—and practicing—this most sacred of all abilities that lives within us all but is often hidden makes the differences between mediocre and good as well as good and great leaders.

LISTENING IN BUSINESS

The bottom line on listening is this—it's one of the most important skills leaders should have, and yet it's often one of the least developed. If you've ever listened to people at work "talk at" each other, you've experienced what I call the talking duel. Each person is fighting the other for air time. Rather than listen to each other and comment or reflect on what the other person is offering to the conversation, instead each person is thinking, rehearsing, and waiting for an opening—a pause in the conversation—to jump in with his or her own "two cents."

Thus, rather than a collaboration or a synchronized dance, conversation looks much more like a contest, even a duel, about who will dominate the conversation. We've gotten the value of listening and the time spent practicing it all out of proportion.

That's important to realize, because in the *Forbes* magazine 2013 article, "6 Ways Effective Listening Can Make You A Better Leader," Glenn Llopis offers the following:

- We have learned 85% of what we know through listening.
- Humans generally listen at only a 25% comprehension rate.
- In a typical business day, we spend 45% of our time listening, 30% of our time talking, 16% reading, and 9% writing.
- Fewer than 2% of all professionals have had formal education on understanding and improving listening skills and techniques.

In a piece titled "Research Behind Listening: **LISTENING FACTS**," Laura Janusik, Ph.D., Rockhurst University, with assistance from Lynn Fullenkamp and Lauren Partese, has compiled some interesting well-documented research data on listening.[27] Here are some key points from that research.

LISTENING—GENERAL

- Listening is an important component in how people judge communicative competence in the workplace.

- Further, individual performance in an organization is found to be directly related to listening ability or perceived listening effectiveness.
- In a spoken message, 55% of the meaning is translated nonverbally, 38% is indicated by the tone of voice, while only 7% is conveyed by the words used.

LISTENING AND LEADERSHIP

- Listening is tied directly to effective leadership.
- The most effective leaders are able to paraphrase the speaker to ensure understanding of the speaker's message.
- Leaders listen with an open mind by not becoming emotional or defensive. Furthermore, strong leaders asked to keep something confidential do not betray the confidence.

LISTENING STYLES

- People listen through one of four primary styles: people-oriented, time-oriented, action-oriented, and content-oriented listening. Females are more likely to be people-oriented listeners and males are more likely to be time-, action-, or content-oriented.
- Victims of major life stressors are often exposed to the following responses from others: (a) inappropriate responses (e.g., minimization, criticizing); (b) a failure to express concern, empathy, or affection; and (c) avoidance from one or more network members (including medical professionals).
- Similarly, support providers have a greater tendency to want to solve problems rather than to engage in supportive listening behaviors. In other words, informal help-providers may avoid listening to the distressed person, which makes the distressed person feel worse rather than better.

- The two most "helpful" listening behaviors when interacting with the bereaved include (1) giving them the opportunity to ventilate, and (2) being fully present.
- Supporters who are effective listeners provide more direct eye contact, are receptive to disclosures, and ask more follow-up questions.

LISTENING AND HEALTHCARE

- Physicians interrupt 69% of patient interviews within 18 seconds of the patient beginning to speak. As a result, in 77% of the interviews, the patient's true reason for visiting was never elicited.
- Patients are less likely to sue practitioners with good bedside manners. In fact, two-thirds of all malpractice cases were tied to breakdowns in communication. Thus, medical practitioners with better communication skills were less likely to be involved in malpractice cases. Patients are dissatisfied with the way that physicians communicate, citing them as lacking concerns and empathy.
- Healthcare practitioners who use more patient-centered communication, including listening, have patients who are more satisfied with their practitioners and their overall medical care.

HOW TO LISTEN

Sometimes the advice given about becoming a better listener is "Just listen!" Sounds simple—and at its core listening is simple—but it takes presence, technique, and practice.

PRESENCE

As mentioned previously, the one gift leaders can give others is their presence—to be completely present and ready to be there, completely there, with another person. When leaders project their presence with eye contact and a smile—signaling that the other person is important—the game changes for both leaders and the person with whom they're communicating.

Famed country western singer and sometimes-philosopher June Carter Cash once said: "I'm just trying to matter." And when we're listened to intently, especially by an authority figure, we "matter" and thrive.

The act of listening is simple but difficult for many executives, who so often work under intense pressure and at uncontrolled speed.

TECHNIQUE

How we listen also matters. For example, if leaders are on the phone talking and scanning email at the same time, that's not being present. It's a kind of hovering, as if they're getting ready to take off! It doesn't count in the world of being totally present and listening.

We all pick up subtle voice changes, inflections, and intonations, and we can often detect when someone's not fully listening to us but is mentally somewhere else. Perfunctory vocalizations like "ahha, ahha," and "yep, yep," are often interpreted as "Can you just move it along?!" That's hardly being present to the person speaking.

If you find yourself in a situation requiring good listening skills, here's one simple technique you can use: the "Speaker-Listener Technique." Often used by the best communicators, psychiatrists, negotiators, and others who have to communicate in difficult situations, this powerful technique is appropriate and effective in any conversation where listening is critical—which, for leaders, should be most of them. The technique is about making any conversation constructive, clear, and safe. It can be used especially well in conflict or in any conversation where you want to support and really communicate with the other person.

This speaker-listener technique was developed and is taught at the Center for Marital and Family Studies at the University of

Denver by three prominent psychologists and professors (Howard J. Markman, Scott M. Stanley, and Susan L. Bloomberg) and explained in detail in their bestselling book, *Fighting for Your Marriage.*[28] And while developed for marriage, this technique provides a powerful listening technique for any leader. What follows is a brief overview of the technique.

General Rules for the Speaker-Listener Technique:

- The speaker is center stage. Whoever is speaking has a chance to be heard and not be interrupted.
- Take turns—a good conversation shares "air time."
- Don't try to fix the problem or issue—this is about hearing and understanding, *not solving*, the problem.

Speaker Guidelines

- Keep it short and sweet—avoid long rambling monologues.
- Know that you're speaking for yourself, not for all of humanity.
- Don't monopolize—leave some space for the listener to jump in.

Listener Guidelines

- Stay engaged. Look at the speaker, nod, encourage using positive gestures.
- Focus on the issue. The listener's primary job is to figure out the speaker's "real" issue. Oftentimes, even the speaker doesn't know what the real issue is!
- Paraphrase. This is critical to both the listener and the speaker. Getting the issue or problem straight before ever attempting to solve it (much later) is the most critical part of this technique. The essence of this conversation is for both speaker and listener to figure out what's really bothering the speaker.

Note: In the story that follows this part of the book, there is a speaker–listener dialogue played out to demonstrate how such a conversation might actually sound.

PRACTICE

Like anything you want to get good at, listening requires effort and practice. It's a bit like using your left hand to eat with if you're right-handed. It takes a lot of practice.

I hurt my right shoulder once, and my doctor suggested I start using my computer mouse with my left hand for a month or two. I thought it was impossible, but within a few weeks I was doing well. Today, I'm pretty much ambidextrous—when it comes to the mouse. Shaving left-handed is next. Gulp!

The good news is that you can practice listening many times a day. Just put other people's stories center stage and ask them questions. In short, get curious about them.

To demonstrate this practice, I conduct an exercise with corporate students called "TV Reporter." I ask them to pair off and interview each other as if they are reporters who will have to deliver a one-minute stand-up broadcast on a simulated live TV news hour. The "reporters" are asked to find out what the "interviewees" did yesterday—and report back on a "Day in the Life of..." the interviewee. After they interview each other, I actually make them stand up and report to an imaginary TV camera. This pressure focuses them to be curious about the other person and gather facts for their report.

THE LADDER OF INFERENCE

Before leaving the topic of listening, it's important to understand the research of Harvard's Chris Argyris on the "Ladder of Inference." Essentially, when we listen, we also tend to hear an internal narrative we create for ourselves based on observations, beliefs, and emotions. This narrative often does not serve us well, but it happens frequently. Here's an example of how the "ladder" works:

Joe is presenting his proposal to the CEO and fellow senior executives in his company. He's getting a lot of attention from everyone except the CFO, Harry. Joe observes Harry, who seems distracted, frequently checking both his iPhone and his watch. Finally, Harry stands up and leaves without a word. This rattles Joe, who cuts his presentation short and rushes to finish without making the key observations he had wanted to make. As he takes his seat, Joe is fuming, convinced that Harry has sabotaged his presentation intentionally. Joe begins plotting payback for Harry, who has to present his budget in an upcoming meeting.

Here's what happened:

1. Joe sees Harry checking his watch and phone. [Registers observable data]
2. Joe concludes that Harry is bored. [Adds meaning]
3. Joe now assumes Harry's trying to torpedo Joe's presentation. [Makes assumptions based on meaning that Joe added about Harry]
4. Joe concludes that Harry is a jerk.
5. Joe decides to attack Harry next week in his presentation. [Intends to take action based on beliefs]
6. Joe might even wait a week or two to observe Harry, but Joe's prejudices will filter and allow in what most supports his belief that Harry is a jerk—also called the confirmation bias—and creates a vicious cycle. [Creates the reflexive loop]

By the way, the real reason Harry was checking his watch and left the meeting is that his wife had called early and said she was taking their son to the emergency room. She told Harry to go to his meeting and would call him with an update as soon as she knew the results of the X-rays!

This scene is repeated in virtually every company and organization that has ever existed on the face of the earth, and is a perfect example of the ladder of inference. Here's how it works in general: We make an observation, jump to a conclusion, support it with future observations biased in favor of a previous conclusion, and take actions based on a narrative we have created and told ourselves.

What are some actions you can take to prevent jumping to often hurtful and harmful conclusion?

1. Verify your assumptions—ask the other person what's going on. Most of the time, it's not at all consistent with story you're telling yourself.
2. Assume that your interpretations are wrong and try to support another theory or explanation of the situation. This helps you avoid confirmation bias.
3. Test your assumptions and selected data with others you trust to see if they concur with the story you're telling yourself.
4. Withhold judgment until you get sufficient concrete data.

Now, back to the story: Strategic Partners.

———

THE STORY ~ ACT 3: LISTEN.

J.C. cleared his throat. "So, let's turn to the last of The 3 Mindful Acts: Listen."

He then announced a concept called the Speaker-Listener Technique. "It's about creating a safe place to admit that you're vulnerable," he said.

"Vulnerability is seen as weakness in business and certainly not what they teach in MBA programs," Mark said with some authority.

"I hear you, Mark. And think how well so many of those relationships work?"

"Fair point! My MBA program was way more than competitive—just this side of hostile!" Mark said, and smiled.

J.C. explained that the Speaker-Listener Technique was developed by professors at a family and marriage counseling institute, and that it has been used successfully in many interpersonal relationships. The point of such conversations was not to solve problems but to be listened to and heard. Having a solid communication structure helps make difficult conversations easier. Basically the speaker has the floor. It's the speaker's job to explain the problem to the listener. The listener's job is to ask questions —not trying to solve the problem, but just being able to paraphrase the real problem back to the speaker, who often does not fully appreciate the core problem until in conversation with a curious, intentional listener.

Then J.C. showed Mark and Sophia a video of a couple, Jack and Sandy, disagreeing with each other, then remembering to use the Speaker-Listener Technique. Here's what the video conversation sounded like:

Jack: Whenever your sister comes to town and tells us how to take care of your Dad, it makes me crazy.

Sandy: You've never liked my sister, admit it.

Jack: Oh, come on. Here we go again. I like her fine, just not how she rides in and out of town on her high horse offering us unsolicited advice.

Sandy: Wait. Let's both take a breath here. We're both getting heated. Let's use the Speaker-Listener Technique that we learned about in marriage counseling.

She walks to the kitchen to get the purple pen—their symbol of who has the floor and the right to speak—and places it on the table between them. Jack takes the pen and acts as the Speaker.

Jack: OK. My real problem with the situation is that I see how hard you work to make your Dad comfortable, and then she swoops in with observations and suggestions without having been involved in the day-to-day work you do.

Sandy: So you're concerned for me—is that it?

Jack: Partly. I know how hard you work at it. And, I resent your sister's unsolicited help. It's like she's an interloper. She comes in with gifts and advice and then flies home, leaving us with the work. I don't like that at all.

Sandy: So you resent her coming with suggestions and not knowing all we do already. Is it like she's coming in like the hero on a white horse?

Jack: Exactly. Here, you take a turn as the Speaker [he hands her the pen].

Sandy: I feel like my sister can't be involved in the day-to-day but feels like she has to contribute. After all, she's a project manager by trade–

Jack [interrupting Sandy]: But does she…. Oops. I'm sorry for talking without the pen and interrupting you.

Sandy: OK…anyway, I think she does the best she can.

Jack: So, you think that she wants to contribute in a meaningful way?

Sandy: Yes, but also I think she believes, and I do too, that she does have some very good ideas. Remember when she helped us out with that Medicare paperwork? So, I'm just saying, I don't want to throw the baby out with the bathwater.

Jack: So, I should listen to her?

Sandy: Wait. Do you want the pen back again?

Jack [blushing]: Not yet, sorry. I need to do a better job as the Listener. So, you think we need to hear her out because she has an emotional need to be a part of the care of your Dad and that she really does have some good ideas? Is that accurate?

Sandy: I'm not trying to solve the problem, just making a couple of observations.

Jack: Great. Thanks. [The conversation ends with them smiling and hugging.]

"OK. That's the technique, and we're almost out of time," J.C. said. "So here's what I want you both to do before we meet again."

He handed Mark and Sophia a piece of paper listing the rules for the Speaker–Listener Technique so they could use it to guide the practice he was going to assign.

J.C. explained that before they use it on a tough, emotional disagreement, they should first practice the technique by discussing something they care about but in which they are not heavily emotionally invested. And, whatever they discuss should not be about their professional relationship.

"So, no discussions about family, money, politics either!" J.C. said.

Then he explained that they might want to discuss a book, sports, or even a movie they really liked or disliked. He told them to do the practice sessions for about 15 minutes and pay attention to the Speaker-Listener Technique. And when they were done practicing on "soft-ball" topics and felt comfortable with the technique, to try using it on one of their milder conflicts. Eventually, they would use the technique to attack tough issues.

They both asked a couple of clarifying questions but eventually agreed to try the Speaker-Listener Technique before the next joint session.

A couple of weeks went by. The individual coaching sessions went well. Mark had the most trouble with the Speaker-Listener Technique, tending to talk too much. At times what he said sounded almost like a lecture. Sophia was a more natural communicator and liked to listen as much as speak. For her, this technique was as easy as taking a walk in the park.

When it was time for the partner session with J.C., they both arrived on time and smiling.

"Ok, hearing from both of you in your individual meetings, if I count it up right you've had about four to five Speaker-Listener conversations," J.C. said. "That about right?"

"Five," Mark said, checking his journal.

Sophia just laughed and shrugged her shoulders.

"So, today I want to try a more difficult conversation. You both willing?"

They nodded.

"Can we talk about one of the client situations that started this coaching?"

Again, a nod, somewhat slower than the first one.

"Mark, would you be the Speaker?"

The conversation went well, with only a couple of rough spots when Mark tried to debate the issue of how he only got testy with people when they didn't listen to him. When he said that Sophia looked at J.C. and they both laughed.

Mark looked quizzical. "What?"

J.C. responded. "Mark, maybe it's about sometimes you want to be the Speaker when you need to be the Listener."

"Like now," Sophia said with a big grin.

Mark got it and returned her smile. "OK. Guess that's why they call it the Speaker-Listener Technique—someone has to listen!"

Over the next six months, J.C. continued to meet once a month with each of them and together with them once a month. The meetings had become productive, fun, and informative. Their partnership had been going very well, and they worked together on serving a number of new clients. In their last meeting, J.C. asked them to list a few things of value that they had gotten from the coaching experience.

As usual, Mark offered to go first. He learned three things:

1. Smiling changes your frame of mind, and it's catching.
2. Breathing is good for more than just getting oxygen!
3. Listening is not a sign of weakness but of real strength.

Next, Sophia took a turn. She offered her list:

1. Smiling is something kids do naturally, and we'd do well to learn from them.
2. Mindful breathing is the key to clear thinking and better decisions.
3. Listening is the most powerful gift a leader can give anyone.

J.C. listened and nodded as they both laid out their lists. At that moment, he felt both proud and satisfied that he'd done well by his clients, and it was time for them to "graduate."

"I am so proud of you both that it's hard to put it words," J.C. said. "So, let me just say 'Thank You' for both for working so hard this past year."

He then stood up to give them a group hug and said in kind of a mock preacher-like voice, "Now go forth and Smile. Breathe. Listen!"

KEY TAKEAWAYS FROM ACT 3: LISTEN.

- Listening is a skill possessed by the very best leaders.
- Listening represents an important gift that every leader can give—a leader's time and attention are highly valued.
- Listening consists of presence, technique, and practice.
- The Speaker-Listener Technique focuses on the listener fully understanding the speaker.
- The Ladder of Inference demonstrates how anyone, including leaders, can jump to conclusions based on their own often erroneous assumptions and beliefs.
- Despite a prodigious amount of data and statistics about how important listening is, leaders often have poor listening skills.
- Listening skills seem to be consistently underdeveloped in all professions, including medicine and business.
- Unfortunately, the prognosis for people becoming more focused, better listeners is not good based on the technical intrusions (emails, texts, etc.) vying for our immediate attention.
- Presence gets demonstrated when leaders are fully engaged, focused, and not distracted when talking to people.

REFLECTION AND PRACTICE

- **Answer these questions:**
  - When you listen to people, how present are you? A lot? A little?
  - How well does your boss listen when you speak?
  - In conversations, do you tend to mostly talk, or mostly listen?
  - In a conversation, are you curious about what the other person is saying, or just waiting for your turn to talk?
  - Would most people call you a good, fair, or poor listener?
  - Have you ever jumped to conclusions based on your own assumptions? What was the result?

- **Try these simple exercises:**
  - First try to understand, then try to be understood.
  - Practice putting the other person's story first in a conversation.
  - Pretend that you're a reporter and will have to do a stand-up report on what you just heard during your conversation. How does this change your listening?
  - Force yourself to repeat back the essence of a story to the person who's telling it to you, to show that you really got it.
  - Try the Speaker-Listener Technique with someone you're comfortable with.
  - When you feel yourself starting to get upset and jumping to conclusions, STOP. Take time to verify with others and make more observations. Move away from an emotional response to a more neutral "judge" persona, objectively hearing the facts of a case.

- **Jot down any thoughts or questions that came from having read this chapter.**
  - _____
  - _____
  - _____
  - _____

CONCLUSION

S mart leaders work out regularly to have a healthy body. They go to the gym, go for a walk or a run, and do all manner of exercise to keep themselves physically fit. In a very similar way, there are three critical activities, which I call "The 3 Mindful Acts," that ensure a kind of quality leadership fitness: smiling authentically, breathing mindfully, and listening intently. These three activities constitute a simple, research-based, and powerful set of mindful acts that make the difference between an average and a great leader. Such acts elevate a leader from success to significance— i.e., having an impact on themselves and more importantly, on others whom they lead.

Be assured, leaders have an easier time performing The 3 Mindful Acts when things are going well. However, those same leaders must perform them when the going gets tough. I'm reminded of Teddy Roosevelt's "Man in the Arena" speech. I present it here out of deep respect for all leaders or parents who manage to smile when hurting and aching to the core; who breathe and act mindfully when their hearts are racing; and who listen when the urge to explain is almost overwhelming. This one's for you:

"It is not the critic who counts; not the man who points out how the strong man stumbles, or where the doer of deeds could have done them better. The credit belongs to the man who is actually in the arena, whose face is marred by dust and sweat and blood; who strives valiantly; who errs, who

comes short again and again, because there is no effort without error and shortcoming; but who does actually strive to do the deeds; who knows great enthusiasms, the great devotions; who spends himself in a worthy cause; who at the best knows in the end the triumph of high achievement, and who at the worst, if he fails, at least fails while daring greatly, so that his place shall never be with those cold and timid souls who neither know victory nor defeat."

OTHER BOOKS BY STEVE GLADIS

POSITIVE LEADERSHIP: THE GAME CHANGER AT WORK

This book provides key research-based principles that will help you be a more effective leader. The first part of the book, "The Concept," gathers some of the best positive psychology research available and reads like a *Harvard Business Review* article. The second part, "The Story," is a leadership fable about a homeless, former business executive who attempts to climb back into society after a shocking body blow to his life. The research and the story together make a memorable read.

THE COACH-APPROACH LEADER

This book is a leadership fable about an elderly businessman, Leon Bausch, who takes over a company and teaches the company about the coaching process as the ultimate leadership model. With the help of Leon's longtime friend, confidant, and executive coach, J.C. Williams, Leon teaches his executives how to help people solve their problems by asking them key questions and by determining the Issue, the Impact, the Ideal, and the Intention. This inspiring leadership story allows the reader to absorb the backbone-solid content of the coaching process by attaching it to a heartfelt story.

THE AGILE LEADER

A leadership fable, *The Agile Leader* is the story of a leader, Luke Hopkins, who leads a national sales team. As he starts making changes and drives his team to achieve corporate sales goals, he runs right into the common conflicts, resistive culture, and company politics that all leaders must navigate to be successful. A former standout college quarterback, Luke seeks out his old football coach, Coach Danforth (Coach D) only to find out that he's died. However, his daughter Allison was given the Coach's last "Playbook for Leaders." She and Luke strike up a strong friendship, and using the tenets Coach D. wrote about (and illustrated with diagrams), Luke learns timely lessons for navigating the complex world of corporate America. Any new or experienced leader reading this book will clearly recognize all the challenges that Luke faces as he tries to make a difference.

THE TRUSTED LEADER

The Trusted Leader is a business fable about a new young leader, Carlos Lopez, who gets promoted to supervising his peers. He gets conflicting advice from his boss about how to take charge, and it backfires. Confused, Carlos seeks out the best leader he's ever known, Coach Jack Dempsey. The two agree to meet regularly at a local restaurant to talk about leadership. The Coach teaches Carlos about how to lead, while Carlos and the coach learn about each other's secret, sad, but ultimately formative pasts. Finally, the coach teaches Carlos about the Trust Triangle—the critical key to leadership.

THE TRANSPARENT LEADER

Written as a business leadership fable, *The Transparent Leader* is the story of a smart emerging leader, Stephanie Marcus, as she navigates the challenging world of business. Fortunately, she meets Lou Donaldson, who acts as a friend, informal coach, and mentor as he guides Steph through the complicated business ecosystem in which she finds herself. Throughout the story, Steph learns about clear leadership communication. She adapts and changes and becomes a more transparent—clear and open—leader. At the same time, she learns Lou's personal story, which helps her fully appreciate his wisdom. An especially good read for women in leadership positions.

THE EXECUTIVE COACH IN THE CORPORATE FOREST

A business fable, *The Executive Coach in the Corporate Forest* is the story of a young, gifted executive coach, J. C. Williams, and his coaching relationships with his rather varied and interesting business clients—all with their own challenges. The book offers some engaging stories, has believable characters with realistic problems, and illustrates the structure and content of the coaching process. The book is a quick read and was written to explain the coaching process to executives who didn't understand it.

THE JOURNEY OF THE ACCIDENTAL LEADER

The Journey of the Accidental Leader is a business fable about a young man who, like so many people, gets thrust into a leadership position he neither wanted nor asked for. What he does and how he reacts makes the book both entertaining and informative. This book is based on the author's practical leadership experience as a Marine Corps officer in Vietnam.

SURVIVAL WRITING FOR BUSINESS

To write well, you need to keep it clear and concise. This book shows how and is a no-nonsense, virtual lifeline to writing success.

THE MANAGER'S POCKET GUIDE TO PUBLIC PRESENTATIONS

This book is an indispensable reference for managers and executives who find themselves in the unfamiliar and often frightening position of having to give a public presentation. It is a compendium of tips that will help any manager learn the survival tactics of public speaking. A simple, quick read, based on the accepted theory and practice of rhetoric, it is also a confidence builder that will help any manager begin to overcome anxiety over public speaking.

THE MANAGER'S POCKET GUIDE TO EFFECTIVE WRITING

Written communication is prevalent at most levels of business, but especially at the managerial level. Your writing may be grammatically and logically sound, but is it effective? Is it conveying your message with the concision and accuracy that makes you an effective communicator? Whether you're a manager in charge of a group of writers, or just a person interested in improving his or her writing skills, *The Manager's Pocket Guide to Effective Writing* uses easy, practical, how-to steps to help you write better and ultimately make a better impression on others.

WRITETYPE: PERSONALITY TYPES AND WRITING STYLES

Based on individual personality styles, this book's content provides new strategies for the four basic types of writers: the correspondent, the technical writer, the creative writer, and the analytical writer. Each person fits one of these well-defined writing "types." Once readers learn their writing personality and follow the writing process suggested in the book, they find writing easier and less anxiety producing.

CONTACT INFORMATION

E-mail:	sgladis@stevegladis.com
Telephone:	703.424.3780
Location:	The George Mason Enterprise Center 4031 University Dr., Suite 100, Fairfax, VA 22030
Website:	www.stevegladisleadershippartners.com
Leadership Blog:	Survival Leadership http://survivalleadership.blogspot.com
Twitter:	@SteveGladis

ABOUT THE AUTHOR

Steve Gladis, Ph.D.
A leadership speaker, author, and executive coach, **Dr. Steve Gladis** is an authority on the subject of leadership. CEO of Steve Gladis Leadership Partners—a leadership development company—he is the author of 19 books on leadership and a professor at George Mason University. His company works with businesses, associations, and U.S. government agencies, and he speaks regularly at conferences and corporate gatherings. A former faculty member at the University of Virginia, Dr. Gladis also served as an FBI special agent and was a decorated officer in the U.S. Marine Corps. His company donates a significant portion of corporate profits back to the community. His previous book, *Positive Leadership: The Game Changer at Work,* is available on Amazon.

REFERENCES

1. The Karate Kid. Internet Movie Database (IMBD). Retrieved November 22, 2015, from http://www.imdb.com/title/tt0087538/

2. Boyatzis, R.E., & McKee, A. (2005). *Resonant Leadership*. Boston: Harvard Business Press.

3. Maxwell, J.C. (2004). *The Journey from Success to Significance*. Nashville, TN: Thomas Nelson Incorporated.

4. Gladis, S. (2013). *Positive Leadership: The Game Changer at Work*. Fairfax, VA: CreateSpace Publishing.

5. Dev, C., & O'Connor, P. (2015, December). *Case Study: Challenge the Middlemen*. Harvard Business Review, 119.

6. Gutman, R. (2011, March). *Ron Gutman: The Hidden Power of Smiling*. TED Talk. Retrieved on November 22, 2015, from https://www.ted.com/talks/ron_gutman_the_hidden_power_of_smiling?language=en

7. Gladis, S. (2013). *Positive Leadership: The Game Changer at Work*. Fairfax, VA CreateSpace Publishing.

8. Ibid.

9. Barsade, Sigal. The Ripple Effect: Emotional contagion and its influence on group behavior. Administrative Science Quarterly. December 2002.

10. Gutman, R. (2011, March). *Ron Gutman: The Hidden Power of Smiling.* TED Talk. Retrieved on November 22, 2015, from https://www.ted.com/talks/ron_gutman_the_hidden_power_of_smiling?language=en

11. Kraft, T. L., & Pressman, S. D. (2012). Grin and bear it: The influence of manipulated facial expression on the stress response. Psychological Science, 23(11), 1372–8. Retrieved from http://doi.org/10.1177/0956797612445312

12. Grandey, A. A., Fisk, G. M., Mattila, A. S., Jansen, K. J., & Sideman, L. A. (2005). Is "service with a smile" enough? Authenticity of positive displays during service encounters. *Organizational Behavior and Human Decision Processes, 96*(1), 38–55. Retrieved from http://doi.org/10.1016/j.obhdp. 2004.08.002

13. ——. (N.d.). Seven Ways to Increase Servers' Tips. Retrieved November 22, 2015, from http://scholarship.sha.cornell.edu/cgi/viewcontent.cgi?article=1112&context=articles

14. Fredrickson, B. L. (1998). What good are positive emotions? *Review of General Psychology 2*(3), 300–319. http://dx.doi.org/10.1037/1089-2680.2.3.300

15. Wikipedia. *Smile.* Wikipedia: The Free Dictionary. Retrieved on November 22, 2015, from https://en.wikipedia.org/wiki/Smile

16. Cuddy, A. (2012, June). *Amy Cuddy: Your Body Language Shapes Who You Are.* TED Talk. Retrieved on November 22, 2015, from https://www.ted.com/talks/amy_cuddy_your_body_language_shapes_who_you_are?language=en

17. Rock, D. (2009). *Your Brain at Work.* HarperBusiness.

18. Gilbert, D. (2004, February). *Dan Gilbert: The Surprising Science of Happiness.* TED Talk. Retrieved on November 22, 2015, from https://www.ted.com/talks/ dan_gilbert_asks_why_are_we_happy?language=en

19. Hanson, R., & Mendius, R. (2009). *Buddha's Brain.* Oakland, CA: New Harbinger Publications Incorporated.

20. Ricard, M. (February 2004). *Matthieu Ricard: The Habits of Happiness.* TED Talk. Retrieved from https://www.ted.com/talks/ matthieu_ricard_on_the_habits_of_happiness?language=en

21. Smalley, S.L., & Winston, D. (2010). *Fully Present.* Philadelphia, PA: Da Capo Lifelong Books.

22. Cooper, A. 60 Minutes Special on Mindfulness. Retrieved on November 22, 2015, from https://www.youtube.com/ watch?v=KDxIBQT7F54

23. Gelles, D. (2015). *Mindful Work.* London: Houghton Mifflin Harcourt.

24. ——. (N.d.). The True Cost of Multi-Tasking. *Psychology Today.* Retrieved November 22, 2015, from https://www.psychologyto- day.com/blog/brain-wise/201209/the-true-cost-multi-tasking

25. Harvard Business School. (N.d.). Introverts: The Best Leaders for Proactive Employees. HBS Working Knowledge. Retrieved November 22, 2015, from http://hbswk.hbs.edu/item/ introverts-the-best-leaders-for-proactive-employees

26. Holy Grail. Wikipedia. Retrieved November 23, 2015 from https://en.wikipedia.org/wiki/Holy_Grail

27. Janusik, L. (N.d.). Listening facts. Retrieved November 22, 2015, from http://www.paragonresources.com/library/listen.pdf

28. Markman, H.J. et al. (2010). San Francisco: *Fighting for Your Marriage.* John Wiley & Sons.

31510038R00046